Big-Note Piano

ENCANTO: Music from the Motion Picture Soundtrack

Disney

Original Songs by Lin-Manuel Miranda

ISBN 978-1-70516-916-2

HAL•LEONARD®

Visit Hal Leonard Online at
www.halleonard.com

World headquarters, contact:
Hal Leonard
7777 West Bluemound Road
Milwaukee, WI 53213
Email: info@halleonard.com

In Europe, contact:
Hal Leonard Europe Limited
42 Wigmore Street
Marylebone, London, W1U 2RN
Email: info@halleonardeurope.com

In Australia, contact:
Hal Leonard Australia Pty. Ltd.
4 Lentara Court
Cheltenham, Victoria, 3192 Australia
Email: info@halleonard.com.au

CONTENTS

8 The Family Madrigal

11 Waiting On A Miracle

14 Surface Pressure

18 We Don't Talk About Bruno

25 What Else Can I Do?

28 Dos Oruguitas

22 All Of You

30 Colombia, Mi Encanto

THE FAMILY MADRIGAL

Music and Lyrics by
LIN-MANUEL MIRANDA

With a Latin groove

MIRABEL:

This is our home, __ we've got ev-'ry gen-er-a - tion.

So full of mu - sic, a rhy-thm of ___ its own de-sign...

This is my fam - ily, a per-fect con-stel-la - tion.

So man-y stars, _____ and _____ ev-'ry-bod - y gets to shine.

Whoa, but let's be clear, A - bue - la runs this _____ show. _____

Whoa, she led us here so man-y years a - go, _____ whoa, and ev-'ry year our

fam - i-ly bless-ings ____ grow! There's just a lot _____ you've sim-ply got to know, so...

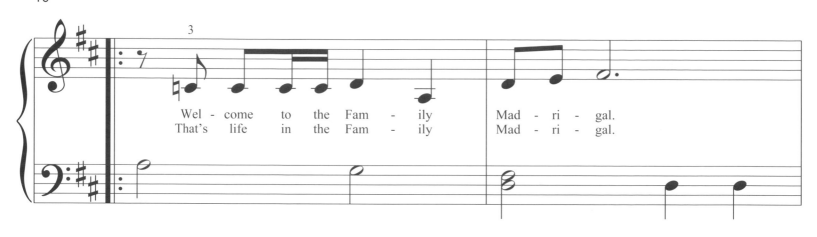

Wel - come to the Fam - ily Mad - ri - gal.
That's life in the Fam - ily Mad - ri - gal.

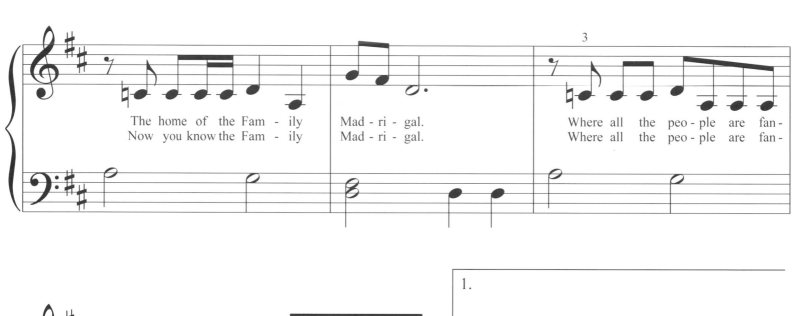

The home of the Fam - ily Mad - ri - gal.
Now you know the Fam - ily Mad - ri - gal.
Where all the peo - ple are fan -
Where all the peo - ple are fan -

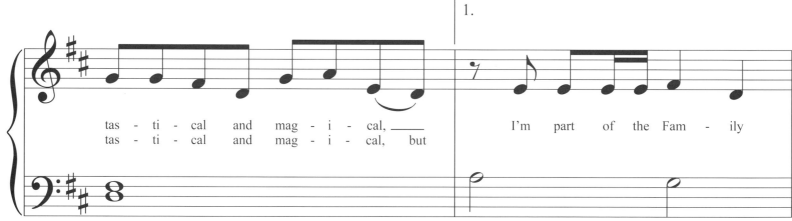

1.

tas - ti - cal and mag - i - cal, _____ I'm part of the Fam - ily
tas - ti - cal and mag - i - cal, but

2.

Mad - ri - gal. that's who we are in the Fam - ily Mad - ri - gal.

WAITING ON A MIRACLE

Music and Lyrics by
LIN-MANUEL MIRANDA

I would move ___ the moun - tains, ___   make new trees ___ and
I would heal ___ what's bro - ken, ___   show this fam - ily

flow - ers grow.   Some - one please ___ just   let me know where do I
some - thing new,   who I am ___ in - side. ___ So what can I

1.
go,   I am wait - ing on a   mir - a - cle, a mir - a - cle.
2.
do? I'm sick of wait - ing on a

Slowly, freely

mir - a - cle, so here I go...   Am I too late for a   mir - a - cle? _____

SURFACE PRESSURE

Music and Lyrics by
LIN-MANUEL MIRANDA

Moderate Pop

mp I'm the strong one, I'm not ner-vous, I'm as tough as the crust of the earth is.
I move moun-tains, I move church-es, and I glow, 'cause I know what my worth is.

I don't ask how hard the work is,

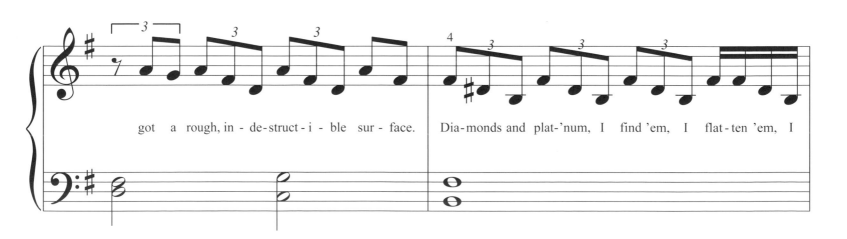

got a rough, in-de-struct-i-ble sur-face. Dia-monds and plat-'num, I find 'em, I flat-ten 'em, I

take what I'm hand - ed, I break what's de - mand - ed, but...

Un - der the sur - face, I feel ber - serk as a tight - rope walk - er in a three - ring cir - cus.

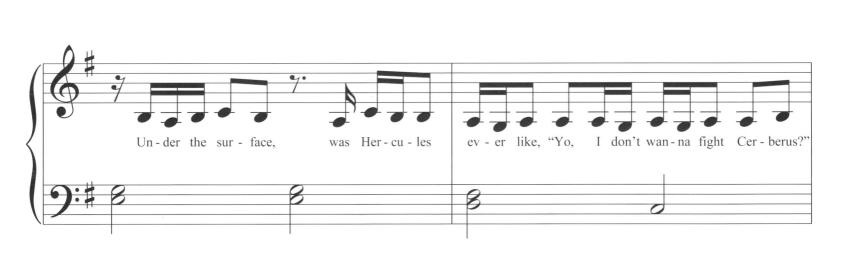

Un - der the sur - face, was Her - cu - les ev - er like, "Yo, I don't wan - na fight Cer - berus?"

Un - der the sur - face, I'm pret - ty sure I'm worth - less if I can't be of ser - vice. A

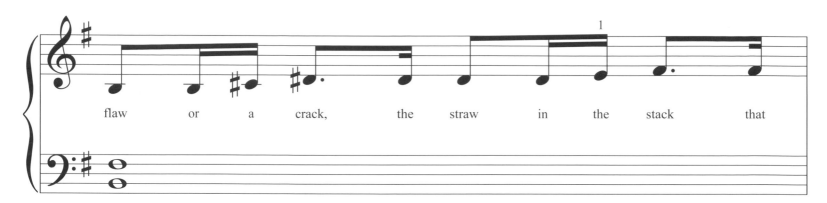

flaw or a crack, the straw in the stack that

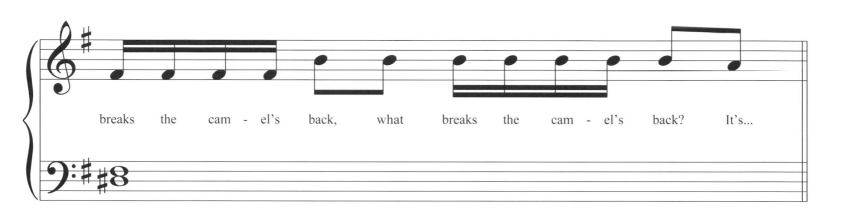

breaks the cam - el's back, what breaks the cam - el's back? It's...

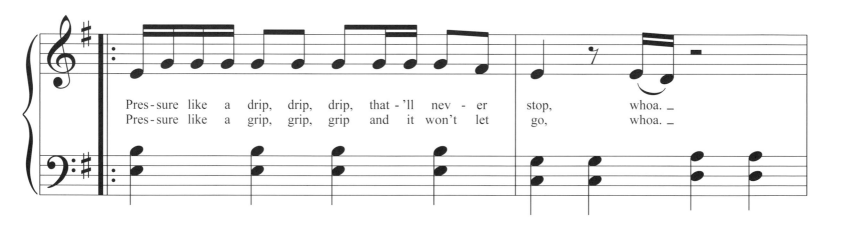

Pres - sure like a drip, drip, drip, that -'ll nev - er stop, whoa.

Pres - sure like a grip, grip, grip and it won't let go, whoa.

Pres - sure that -'ll tip, tip, tip 'til you just go pop, whoa - oh - oh.

Pres - sure like a tick, tick, tick 'til it's read - y to blow, whoa - oh - oh.

Give it to your sis - ter, your sis - ter's old - er,
Give it to your sis - ter, your sis - ter's strong - er,

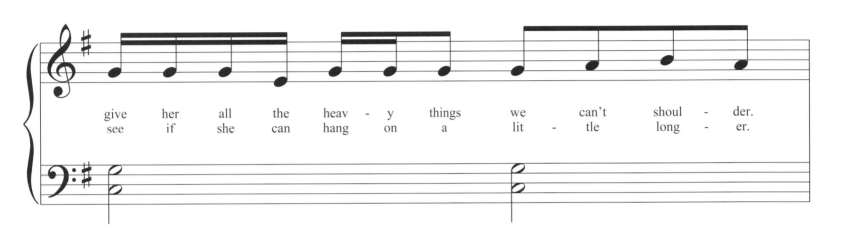

give her all the heav - y things we can't shoul - der.
see if she can hang on a lit - tle long - er.

1.

Who am I if I can't run with the ball? _____ If I fall to...
Who am I if I don't have what it

2.

takes? No cracks, no... breaks, no mis - takes! No pres - sure!

WE DON'T TALK ABOUT BRUNO

Music and Lyrics by
LIN-MANUEL MIRANDA

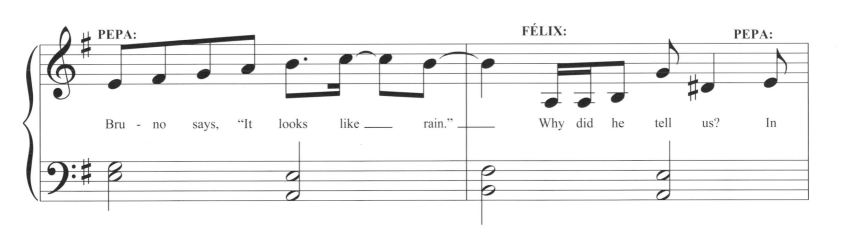

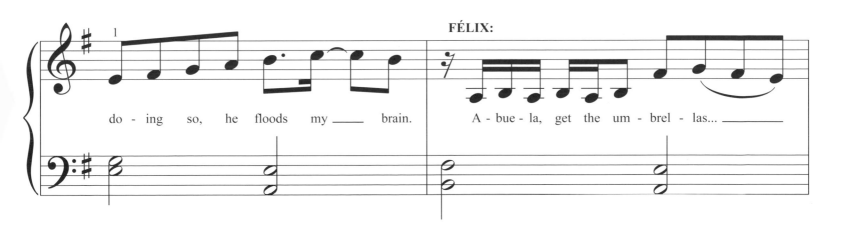

on _____ your screams. We don't talk a - bout Bru -

- no, no, ____ no, no! We don't talk a - bout Bru - no! _____

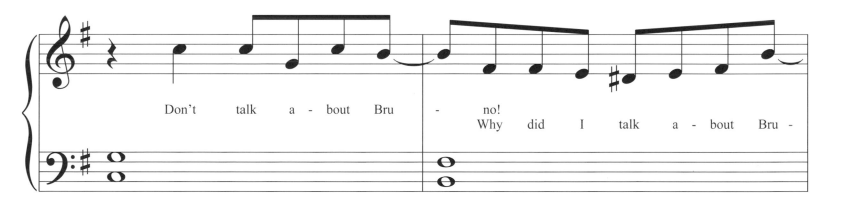

Don't talk a - bout Bru - no! Why did I talk a - bout Bru -

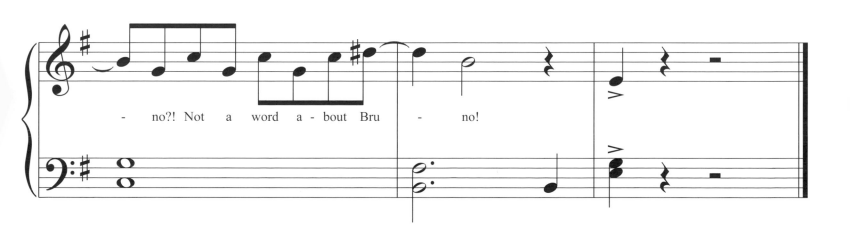

- no?! Not a word a - bout Bru - no!

ALL OF YOU

Music and Lyrics by
LIN-MANUEL MIRANDA

MIRABEL:

Look at this home, we

need a new foun-da - tion. It may seem hope - less, but we'll get by just fine.

Look at this fam - 'ly, a glow-ing con-stel-la - tion

so full of stars, and ev - 'ry-bod - y wants to shine.

But the stars don't shine, ____ they burn, ____ and the

con - stel - la - tions ____ shift. I think it's time ____ you learn: ____

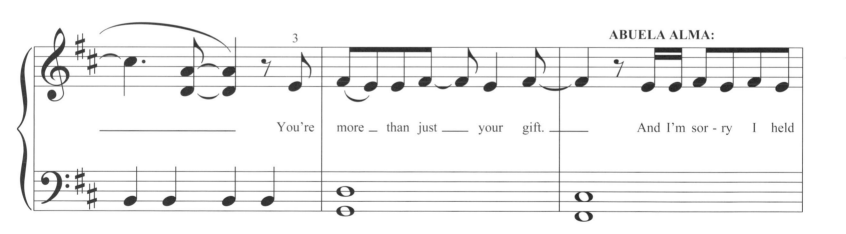

ABUELA ALMA:

____ You're more _ than just ____ your gift. ____ And I'm sor - ry I held

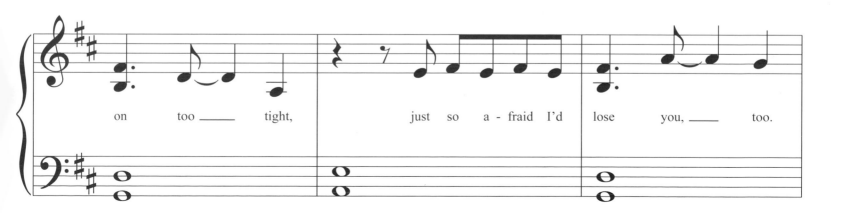

on too ____ tight, just so a - fraid I'd lose you, ____ too.

The mir-a-cle is not some mag-ic that ___ you've got,

the mir-a-cle is you, ___ not some gift, just you... _

add JULIETA & PEPA:

_ The mir-a-cle is you. All of you, ___ all of you. _

MIRABEL, ABUELA ALMA & TOWNSPEOPLE:

All of you, ___ all of you. _

WHAT ELSE CAN I DO?

Music and Lyrics by
LIN-MANUEL MIRANDA

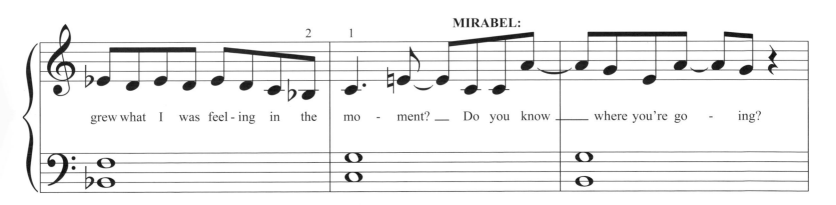

ISABELA:

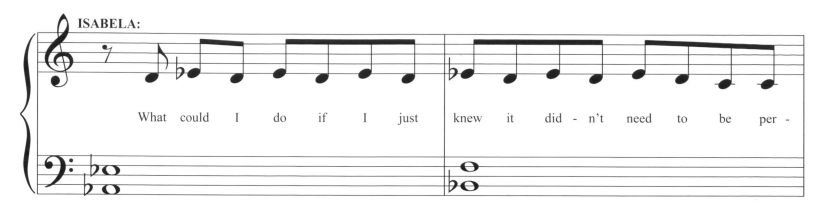

What could I do if I just knew it did - n't need to be per -

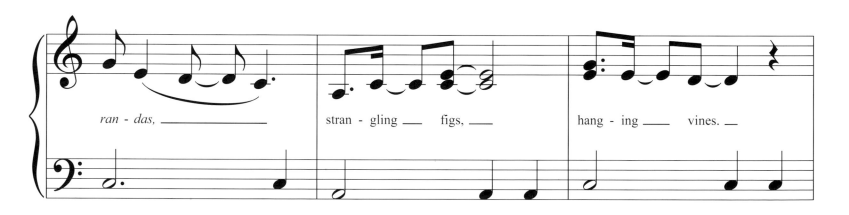

fect, it just need - ed to be? ___ And they let me be? A hur - ri - cane of *ja - ca -*

ran - das, ___ stran - gling ___ figs, ___ hang - ing ___ vines. ___

Pal - ma de ce - ra fills the air as I ___ climb and I push

To Coda

through... What else ___ can I do? ___ What else ___ can I

MIRABEL:

do?
All I know are the blos - soms you grow, but it's awe - some to see ___ how you rise. ___

BOTH:

___ How far ___ can you rise? ___ Through the roof, to the skies, ___

D.S. al Coda

___ let's go... ___

CODA

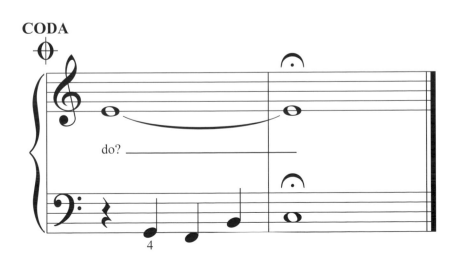

do? ___

DOS ORUGUITAS

Music and Lyrics by
LIN-MANUEL MIRANDA

Syncopated groove

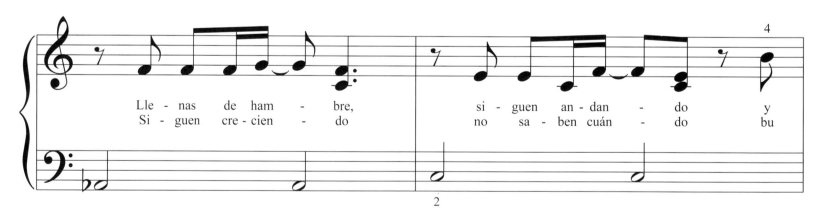

na - ve - gan - do un mun - do que cam - bia y si - gue cam - bian - do.
se - pa - ra - bles son, y el tiem - po si - gue cam - bian - do.

Ay, or - u - gui - tas, no se a - guan - ten más. Hay __ que cre - cer a - part - te y vol - ver,

ha - cia a - de - lan - te se __ gui - rás. Vie - nen mi - la - gros, vien - en cri - sá - li - das.

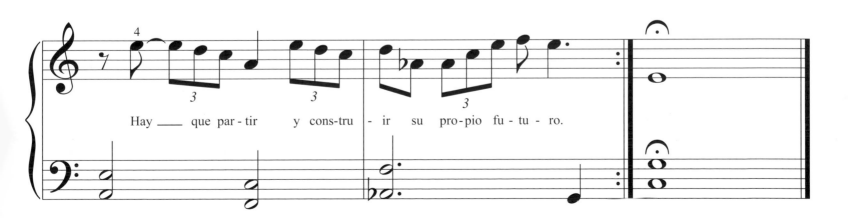

Hay __ que par - tir y cons - tru - ir su pro - pio fu - tu - ro.

COLOMBIA, MI ENCANTO

Music and Lyrics by
LIN-MANUEL MIRANDA

Moderately fast

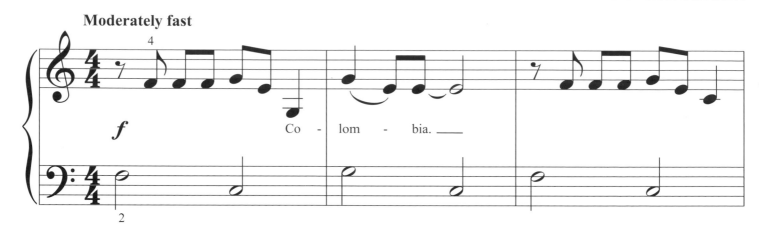

Co - lom - bia.

No - che de fies - ta, to - dos vie - nen a ce - le - brar.

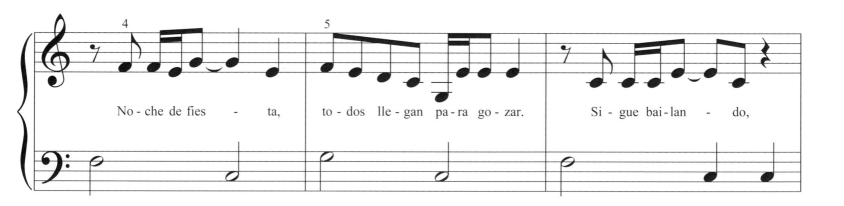

No - che de fies - ta, to - dos lle - gan pa - ra go - zar. Si - gue bai - lan - do,

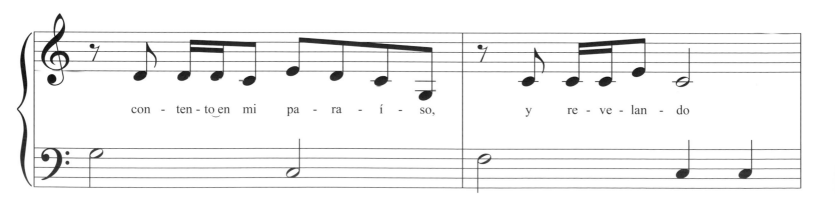

con - ten - to en mi pa - ra - í - so, y re - ve - lan - do

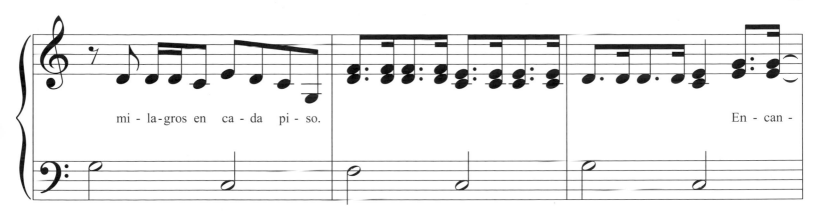

mi - la - gros en ca - da pi - so. En - can -

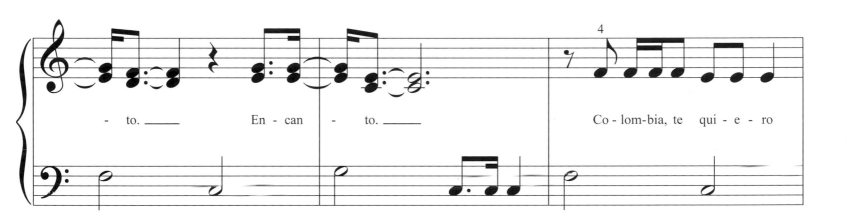

- to. _____ En - can - to. _____ Co - lom - bia, te qui - e - ro

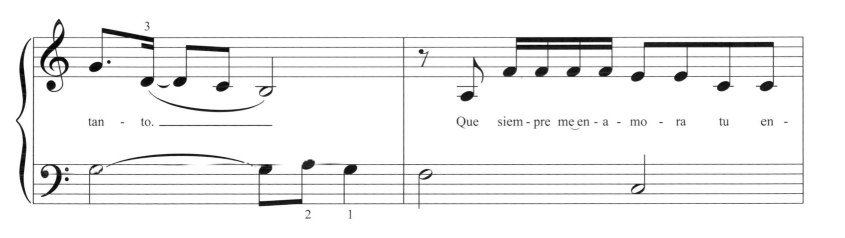

tan - to. _____ Que siem - pre me en - a - mo - ra tu en -

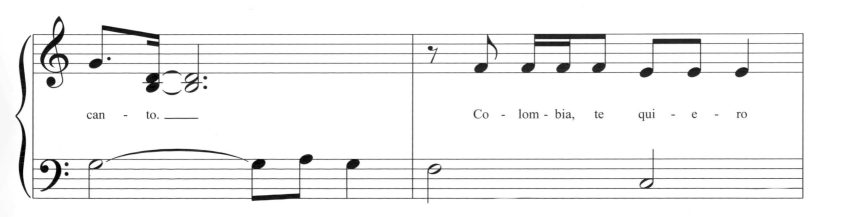

can - to. _____ Co - lom - bia, te qui - e - ro

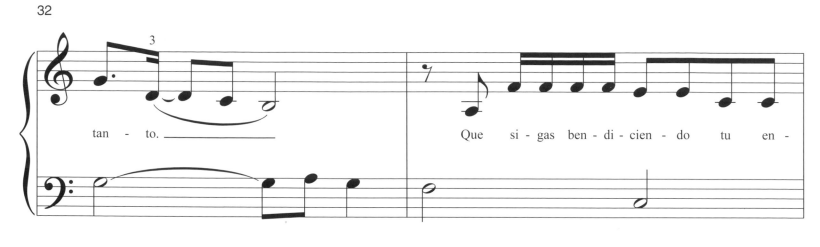

tan - to. _____ Que si - gas ben - di - cien - do tu en -

can - to... ___ Co - lom - bia. ___ En - can

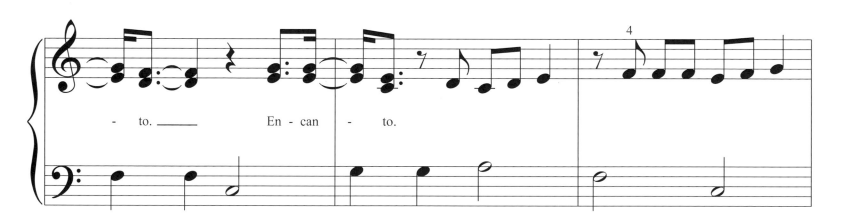

- to. ___ En - can - to. En - can - to.

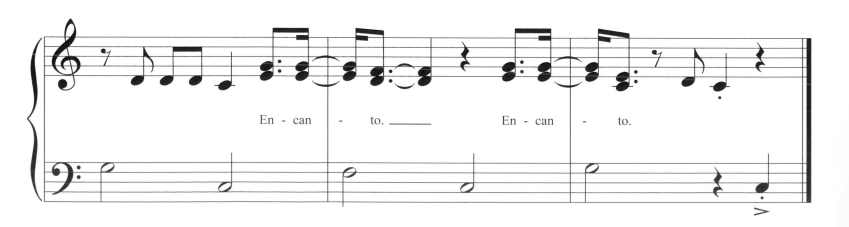

En - can - to. ___ En - can - to.